ROSSENDALE
THEN & NOW

IN COLOUR

SUSAN HALSTEAD

The
History
Press

First published in 2013

The History Press
The Mill, Brimscombe Port
Stroud, Gloucestershire, GL5 2QG
www.thehistorypress.co.uk

British Library Cataloguing in Publication Data.
A catalogue record for this book is available from the British Library.

ISBN 978 0 7524 7144 0

Typesetting and origination by The History Press
Manufacturing managed by Jellyfish Solutions Ltd
Printed in India.

CONTENTS

ACKNOWLEDGEMENTS

With thanks to Lancashire County Council: Rossendale District Libraries for kind permission to reproduce forty-five photographs from library collections.

For their ready willingness to share their local knowledge: Simon Bell, Holchem Laboratories Ltd; Kath Burrows; Nick Bury, District Manager, Rossendale District Libraries; Charles Butterworth; Jimmy Eaton; Haslingden Hearing Centre; Allan Howarth, C.P.A. Social and Bowling Club, Loveclough; Ron Howell, Friends of Rossendale Museum; Tricia Kenny, Community History Manager, Rossendale District Libraries; Gildas Kilgallon; Kershaw Print, Loveclough.

For valuable assistance on reading my manuscript: Stephen Barnes; Ken F. Bowden; Wilfred Day; Philip Dunne; Kathy Fishwick; Trevor C. Halstead; Carol Hoskin (for proofreading the complete manuscript); Owen James; Suzanne Lord (for proofreading the complete manuscript); Lewis Pearson; John Simpson; Carole Watchorn; Whitworth Historical Society.

For continuing friendship and support from the staff of Rossendale District Libraries and Rossendale Museum.

ABOUT THE AUTHOR

Susan Halstead, who lives in nearby Accrington, has always been interested in local history. After working as a Local Studies Librarian for thirty-two years, she is keen to publicise the photographic collections held by public libraries. Her previous titles include *Around Rossendale*.

INTRODUCTION

I wrote *Around Rossendale* in 1996 when I was Reference and Local Studies Librarian at Rawtenstall Library, using photographs from the extensive library collections. When I began writing *Rossendale Then & Now*, it seemed appropriate that I should be working in Rossendale again, albeit for a short time, at Rossendale Museum in Whitaker Park, Rawtenstall.

Firstly, I had to select forty-five photographs from *Around Rossendale* and take the modern equivalent. When I made the original selection, I deliberately chose 'people' photographs, so that newcomers to the area would find the book interesting as social history, portraying a way of life which had long since disappeared. This considerably limited my choice because I needed views of recognisable buildings or roads to make a viable comparison.

The next problem was to find the exact position from where the original photographs were taken – in many cases, a very busy road or junction. I soon discovered that, even though some modern pictures initially looked the same as the nineteenth-century scene, they all reflected the most significant historical development of all, i.e. the number of motor vehicles on our roads with their consequent 'clutter' of road markings and traffic signs.

A complex timetable was required for the best times to take photographs: weekday (fewer parked cars outside residents' homes) or weekend (quieter roads)? Morning or afternoon (depending on the sun's position)? Time of year (no foliage on trees or flowering shrubs)?

Of course, there was always the problem of whether the sun would come out at all in 2012 and the rain stop long enough for me to get the camera ready for action!

I did discover that taking photographs is a good way of meeting people. I have been spotted by many acquaintances standing in the middle of a road with one eye on a good picture and the other on a lorry bearing down on me at great speed! Strangers of all ages view the photographer, especially one with a clipboard and making notes, with curiosity and begin a conversation – an excellent way of finding out about changes in the area.

Research was required to find out what had happened over the years. If a building had disappeared, it could be a lengthy task to trace its demolition date – only for this information to be given in just five words in the caption, e.g. 'X was demolished in 1969'. I was very grateful that my professional career had equipped me with knowledge of the vast range of sources of information available in libraries and online. It is interesting to note that in 1996 I principally used books and newspapers available in the local libraries; this time I found much of the information on the internet but was careful to use official websites and to double check when necessary.

I have tried to make this a story of people's lives, not just a history of the buildings they lived in, and also to show the influence of modern inventions and developments on the urban landscape.

Please note: Information in the captions was correct when each photograph was taken in 2011 or 2012, but additional changes have inevitably taken place, particularly in the usage of buildings, which it has not been possible to incorporate.

BLACKBURN ROAD, HASLINGDEN

A HORSE-DRAWN tower wagon, owned by Accrington Corporation's Cleansing
Department, is outside No. 194 Blackburn Road in 1908 installing overhead wires for the
much newer technology of electric trams. Steam trams had first run from Accrington to
the Commercial Hotel in Haslingden on 27 August 1887, but work on the electrification
process began twenty years later. Haslingden Corporation decided it was uneconomic to
operate its own electric cars, so Accrington Corporation extended their tram service from
Baxenden to Haslingden on 5 September 1908, providing a ten-minute service each way

on Tuesdays, Saturdays and Sundays and every fifteen minutes on other days. Four tramcars were housed overnight in the John Street depot to enable an early morning service to commence from Haslingden but, in July 1916, when it was discovered that a local haulier was renting space there to store waste paper, Accrington officials considered this a serious fire risk and withdrew the trams to garage them in Accrington.

THE MODE OF travel is rather different now on this busy thoroughfare! The electric tramline from Accrington to Haslingden ceased operating in 1930 to be replaced by a motor bus service and the last tram is pictured on page ten. However, the most far-reaching change to the country's bus network took place on 26 October 1986 when responsibility for providing bus services passed from the local authority to commercial bus companies. The bus seen here provides a half-hourly service between Manchester and Blackburn. This timetable would have been an unbelievable prospect in the earliest days of public transport when, according to the *History, directory and gazetteer of the county palatine of Lancaster* by Edward Baines in 1824, there was a stagecoach service from Haslingden to Manchester three times a week setting off at 6 a.m. and returning at 4 p.m.

CARRS, HASLINGDEN

CARRS, *c.* 1930. This attractive hamlet was a popular destination for picnics. Commerce Street runs across the middle of the picture; the ivy-clad house in the middle right on the edge of the photograph is Carr Hall Villa; the cotton mill on the middle left is Carr Hall Mill, which was destroyed by fire in August 1978. The railway line from Stubbins to Accrington can faintly be seen to the right of the long building at the front left belonging to Prinny Hill Steam Rope Works. The East Lancashire Railway Company opened the railway line on 17 August 1848 but it closed on 3 December 1966, followed by unsuccessful investigations into the feasibility of the line being taken over by a private enterprise.

THIS AUTUMNAL SCENE was taken slightly to the right of the original photograph because trees now obscure the view. Plans were published in 1975 for the development of Carrs Industrial Estate and the A56 Haslingden bypass which have replaced this small textile community. Sixty-two houses were demolished in the late 1970s and the bypass, following the course of the former railway line, was officially opened on 4 December 1981 by the then minister for transport, Kenneth Clarke MP. It was hoped that the road would bring new industry to Rossendale and it was welcomed by local people who found it was now safer to cross the roads in the centre of Haslingden. The sandy-coloured industrial units belong to the W.H. Good Group which provides specialist electrical engineering services. The building with a northern lights roof construction cannot be seen on the 1930s photograph but is the former cotton mill, Grove Mill. It closed for textile purposes in December 1959 and is now owned by Warton Metals Ltd, a leading UK independent manufacturer of solder wires and products.

BLACKBURN ROAD AND DEARDENGATE JUNCTION, HASLINGDEN

A LARGE CROWD greets the last electric tram from Accrington on 1 May 1930, driven by the Mayor of Rawtenstall, Alderman W. Hardman. Other officials took on additional driving duties for the day: the last tram from Haslingden to Accrington driven by Captain Baxter had been the first electric car to enter Haslingden from Accrington; and the first bus from Haslingden to Accrington was driven by the Mayor of Haslingden, Councillor W. Halstead.

Note the single-decker motor bus lying in waiting! Policemen on point duty at the junction had frequently found their view of traffic obscured by waiting trams on both sides, so it was hoped that the change to buses would ease traffic congestion. Although Haslingden never ran its own trams, it had been the fourth authority in the country to introduce a motor bus service. This ran to Helmshore intermittently from November 1907 until July 1909, but was unsuccessful as the bus 'has not yet been brought to... a stage of perfection'.

ALTHOUGH THIS JUNCTION is quiet on a Sunday morning, the control of traffic is still a problem and it was necessary to install traffic lights in September 1931, not long after the first automatic traffic lights in Great Britain were installed in Wolverhampton in 1930. The yellow car on the right is passing the gates of Haslingden Market on the site previously occupied by Trinity Baptist Chapel; its attractive façade can be seen in the 1930s photograph. This chapel opened in November 1873, but was demolished in 1969 following its amalgamation the previous year with Ebenezer Baptist Chapel (see page seventeen). The market was transferred from its previous site on Bury Road and was opened officially by the Mayor of Rossendale, Councillor Mollie Disley, on 26 June 1998.

HIGHER DEARDENGATE, HASLINGDEN

KING GEORGE V and Queen Mary visited Haslingden on 9 July 1913 during a 'long and tiring week' in which they asked to see working people and 'the chief industries in which they are employed'. They departed from Lord Derby's home in Knowsley at 9.55 a.m. for the train to Colne and drove through Nelson and Burnley, lunching at Gawthorpe Hall with Lord and Lady Shuttleworth; then onwards to Accrington, Rossendale and Rochdale, departing from there at 6.40 p.m. – a whirlwind tour indeed! On arrival in Haslingden, they were greeted by the Mayor, Alderman J.T. Warburton, who announced a public appeal to raise funds for a motor ambulance

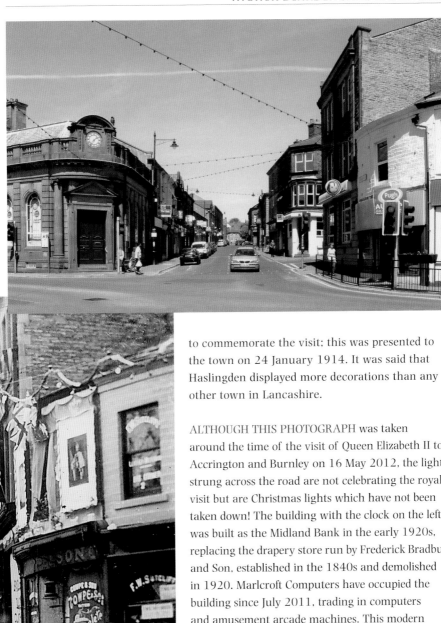

to commemorate the visit; this was presented to the town on 24 January 1914. It was said that Haslingden displayed more decorations than any other town in Lancashire.

ALTHOUGH THIS PHOTOGRAPH was taken around the time of the visit of Queen Elizabeth II to Accrington and Burnley on 16 May 2012, the lights strung across the road are not celebrating the royal visit but are Christmas lights which have not been taken down! The building with the clock on the left was built as the Midland Bank in the early 1920s, replacing the drapery store run by Frederick Bradbury and Son, established in the 1840s and demolished in 1920. Marlcroft Computers have occupied the building since July 2011, trading in computers and amusement arcade machines. This modern technology enables people to enjoy very different types of leisure activities from listening to the gramophone or attending church socials which would have amused the local population in 1913 in the little spare time they had. The display boards advertising shops for sale or to let on a shopping street which was a hub of activity a century ago are a sad reminder of the current decline of town centre shops.

13

LOWER DEARDENGATE, HASLINGDEN

HAROLD YATES RAN his grocery shop from No. 65 Lower Deardengate in 1916. Bird's Custard and 'fresh and pure' Stork Margarine figure prominently in the window displays concentrating on quantity rather than variety! The pavement has been laid with Haslingden Flag which was so exceptionally hardwearing that local quarries also supplied other parts of the country, including Trafalgar Square. This grocer's shop was part of a terraced row built as Greens Buildings in 1850 by John Green. He was born in 1802 and ran a successful family business as a saddler but, by the time these premises were erected, John had lost his first wife Alice, who died at the age of twenty-nine, and seven children, all of whom died under the age of thirteen.

THIS PROPERTY HAS been used for a variety of retail purposes, including selling shoes and as a charity shop, Age Concern, but it has been occupied by a hearing aid service for the past ten years. The door and window frames have been modernised, but the original stone surrounds remain the same. Part of the metal hook is still embedded in the stone sill of the first-floor window but, with greater awareness of the need for better hygienic conditions where food is sold, we no longer see meat suspended in shop doorways. The adjacent District Bank was built in 1914, becoming part of National Westminster in 1970 but closing as a bank in November 2011. The pelican crossing, first introduced in the UK in 1969, is just one of the many modern road safety improvements which have succeeded in reducing the death rate on the roads from 4,886 in 1926 to 1,901 in 2011, even though there are now over 34 million motor vehicles in the country.

HASLINGDEN BAPTIST CHURCH, BURY ROAD

EBENEZER BAPTIST CHAPEL on the corner of Warwick Street before 1899. A breakaway group of fifteen members from Trinity Baptist Chapel on Blackburn Road began meeting in a blacksmith's shop on Pickering Street in 1842, but had attracted enough support three years later to raise the sum of £800 required for this chapel to be built by John Tomlinson.

The congregation continued to grow and fundraising began again in 1887 for another building on the same site, this time at a cost of £5,800. The cornerstones for a more elaborate new chapel, pictured above without its original first storey, were laid on 22 July 1899 by Henry W. Trickett, JP, Mayor of Rawtenstall.

HASLINGDEN BAPTIST CHURCH was created from an amalgamation of Ebenezer and Trinity Baptist Chapels in January 1968 with the congregations meeting in Trinity Chapel whilst the Ebenezer building was prepared. The diamond-shaped 1845 date stone from the top of the original chapel has been incorporated into this building above the window on the left and is balanced on the right by the 1900 date stone. In 1938, the church committee decided to organise a social hour to distract teenagers from their 'Sunday evening street parades'. The church closed in 1978 for radical alterations to reduce heating costs and the upper floor was removed. This much smaller building, re-opened in June 1979, provides a worship area and meeting rooms used for a wide variety of community purposes. At the front left of the church garden is a stone Celtic cross, officially unveiled on Armistice Day 1922 as a memorial to the fifteen men from the chapel and Sunday school who had died in the First World War; another four names were added in June 1947 for those who died in the Second World War.

17

WHITE HORSE INN, HELMSHORE

HOLCOMBE HUNT IN 1926. The hounds used by the hunt are believed to be direct descendants of the Blue Gascoignes, brought across the English Channel by the Normans in the eleventh century. When King George V and Queen Mary visited Lancashire in 1913, the hunt was described as one of the oldest established harrier packs in England. The White Horse Inn was built in 1825 and its innkeeper in 1881, Daniel Barnes, was a man of many commercial interests – a 'farmer of 15 acres, innkeeper and cotton mill manager'. The three semi-detached houses in the process of construction were council houses, built at a cost of £2,970, at a time when it was still the responsibility of the local council to provide well-built homes at reasonable rents.

HOLCOMBE HUNT NO LONGER meets at the White Horse but is still active. It has, however, had to adapt to the requirements of the Hunting Act 2004 outlawing the use of dogs to chase and kill wild animals. The White Horse re-opened as a family-run pub food restaurant in 2010 and the single-storey building on the left, formerly a barn, is here occupied by Paraphernalia, a new shop selling gifts and antiques, even on a Sunday. Opening hours were relaxed by the Sunday Trading Act of 1994 and this has now made the 'day of rest', as it would have been in 1926, a busy shopping day for many working families. The Union Jack outside the shop marks the Diamond Jubilee celebrations for Queen Elizabeth II in June 2012. The houses now have established gardens and also satellite dishes offering a variety of television channels which would have amazed John Logie Baird in 1926 when he gave the world's first demonstration of a working television.

HOLCOMBE ROAD, HELMSHORE

MAYORAL PROCESSION FOR Jerry Lord outside Springhill Wesleyan School in 1926. The foundation stone for this Sunday school was laid on 28 June 1890, but the chapel to the left of the picture had opened on 15 September 1867. Both buildings were central to village life until after the Second World War and were used until an amalgamation with Sion Primitive Methodist Chapel in August 1962. Middle Mill on the right of the picture was built as a woollen mill in 1823/4 by William and Ralph Turner and was significant as the area's first entirely steam-powered factory. By the 1920s, the mill was in difficulties but, the year after this photograph was taken, the share capital had been purchased by J.H. Birtwistle and

Company Limited and 200 workers were employed weaving a wide variety of cloth.

MODERN HOUSES AT Nos 399-401a are now on the site of the school and chapel. The adjacent building was opened on 2 April 1892 as Helmshore Conservative Club by the MP for Dover, George Wyndham, but has been a private home since 1976. Middle Mill closed in 1931 but was renamed as Wavell Works and used for munitions manufacture during the Second World War. The mill finally closed as a textile concern in 1981, becoming the headquarters of the travel company Airtours, until its closure in 2007. It was at one time Britain's biggest package holiday operator taking travellers to destinations all around the world, whereas the textile workers would have been excited about a day trip to Blackpool. The white advertising sign is outside purpose-built offices in Wavell House which replaced the weaving shed, demolished in 1990, and they are now occupied by a bailiffs company at a time when there are much higher levels of personal debt than in the 1920s.

21

GRANE ROAD, HASLINGDEN

FEMALE MEMBERS OF the congregation from St Stephen's Church, Grane, are passing the gates of Haslingden Cemetery on a Walking Day procession, returning to their church (which was built in 1864 on its original site next to Calf Hey Road). The first interment in the cemetery took place on 29 April 1902, the day before the official opening ceremony when a crowd of 1,000 people turned up to mark the occasion, but had to shelter under umbrellas from the 'piercing wind' and 'bitterly cold showers'. The cemetery had been designed by the Borough Surveyor, J. Singleton Green, on 10 acres

of land at a cost of £7,000. The three denominational chapels, designed by Messrs Simpson and Duckworth, Blackburn, were particularly noteworthy because they were built as one building.

LITTLE SEEMS TO have changed in this scene, but St Stephen's Church was the focal point of a close-knit, independent community and has since been moved stone by stone to the site behind the photographer. The Bury and District Joint Water Board, established in 1900, was responsible for providing a reliable water supply for rapidly expanding industrial populations. Its decision to build Ogden Reservoir, which was officially opened in March 1912, required the purchase of land, mills and homes and resulted in the gradual disappearance of Grane as a village. The church was demolished in 1925, but the courses and stones were carefully marked so they could be re-used to build a new church. This was re-consecrated by the Rt Revd Percy Mark Herbert on Sunday, 22 May 1927, soon after his enthronement as the first Bishop of Blackburn in February the same year. The church closed in turn in 1986, but the building is still in use as the Holden Wood antiques showroom and tea room which opened in 1996.

JUBILEE ROAD, HASLINGDEN

A WHITSUNTIDE PROCESSION for St Stephen's Sunday school, Grane, *c.* 1930. The railway line can only faintly be seen in the top right, but the embankment is more clearly visible on the modern photograph and is one of the few surviving remains of the railway network in Rossendale. Both single-storey buildings had been demolished by the early 1960s, but many local people, particularly visitors to the cemetery, remember Jimmy Parkinson selling flowers there from a small green wooden hut. Jimmy was especially memorable for his courage in not giving in to cerebral palsy. Following his maxim, 'I try to overcome it', he travelled daily by bus to Samlesbury to work for seven years in a nursery but, when this proved too difficult, he took over 'The Hut' in 1969. At a time when the London Paralympics 2012 have heightened

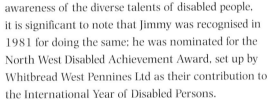

awareness of the diverse talents of disabled people, it is significant to note that Jimmy was recognised in 1981 for doing the same; he was nominated for the North West Disabled Achievement Award, set up by Whitbread West Pennines Ltd as their contribution to the International Year of Disabled Persons.

JIMMY RAN HIS business until his death in 1991 when his mother took it over until 1998. A new building with brightly-coloured cladding was then constructed by Holchem in 1999. Just to the right of the photograph is the property formerly occupied by the Hurstwood Group, but Holchem moved in during 1992 and named it Premier House because the football Premier League was formed the same year. Holchem specialise in industrial cleaning detergents for food factories, breweries, dairies and the hospitality trade and are an expanding business since health and safety regulations are much more extensive now than in 1930. Although Holchem were on the site in May 2012 when this photograph was taken, they were in the process of transferring their business, including buildings on Carrs Industrial Estate, to a new site at Pilsworth in October 2012.

BOWKER STREET, IRWELL VALE

CELEBRATIONS FOR THE village centenary in 1933 included morris dancing in the street, games and a fancy dress parade in the field next to Irwell Vale Methodist Church. On the modern photograph, a date stone inscribed with 'Irwell Vale, 1833' can just be seen on the right, above the first doorway. The street was named after John Bowker who was the founder of Irwell Vale. As a Prestwich merchant, he bought land in the area in 1798 to build the water-powered Hardsough and Irwell Vale Mills and these millworkers' homes, which originally had no back doors. The rents were 1s per week but were increased to 2s 6d when water was supplied and then to 4s 6d to include electricity.

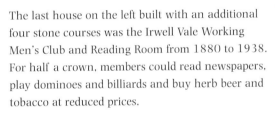

The last house on the left built with an additional four stone courses was the Irwell Vale Working Men's Club and Reading Room from 1880 to 1938. For half a crown, members could read newspapers, play dominoes and billiards and buy herb beer and tobacco at reduced prices.

THE UNION JACKS mark a celebration of a different kind on Bank Holiday Monday, 4 June 2012. A 1940s wartime re-enactment weekend with numerous activities along the course of the railway line from Heywood to Rawtenstall had been organised by the East Lancashire Railway to commemorate the Diamond Jubilee of Queen Elizabeth II. Passengers dressed in 1940s costume have just alighted from the steam train at the Irwell Vale halt, which had been re-opened in 1991, and are hurrying to the Methodist church at the end of the street for refreshments and a tea dance. Irwell Vale was designated a conservation area in the mid-1970s as a good example of a Lancashire mill village, so little has changed in the street except for the presence of the ubiquitous motor vehicle.

BOLTON ROAD NORTH, STUBBINS

THE RAILWAY HOTEL, pictured here around 1905, was so named because it stood next to Stubbins Station and the railway line from Ramsbottom north to Rawtenstall and Accrington. A private siding served Ramsbottom Gas Works behind the terraced row to the front right; the gas light is outside the company offices. The public house was renamed the Corner Pin in the 1970s, but had been known locally by that name for many years. The 'corner pin boys' were well paid block printers from the calico printing Stubbins Print Works, occupied in May 2012 by Georgia-Pacific, a paper manufacturer. They were valued

customers and were given preferential treatment with an area reserved for their own use. In more recent times, this public house has hosted the Official World Black Pudding Throwing Championships which were organised there until 2002.

THE CORNER PIN no longer serves thirsty workers; it closed in May 2003 and has been renovated as offices. The shops with green canopies recall the past with Paul's Corner Shop and Jean's Bakery selling early breakfasts from 6.30 a.m. and 'home made pies and cakes just like Grandma used to make'. However, the wares of some of the shops further up the road would have seemed incredible to local families at the turn of the twentieth century – a tandoori takeaway and Posh Paws, a hairdressing service for dogs 'because dogs need pampering too'. The terraced row to the front right was demolished in the early 1970s and replaced by Cuba Industrial Estate, so named after Cuba Mill located next to the gas works. Cooldelight Desserts Ltd on the estate markets its ice cream and desserts as free from contentious additives and hydrogenated fats; food in 1905 did not contain the numerous additives widely used today to improve shelf life and meals were mostly prepared from local, seasonal ingredients.

MARKET PLACE, EDENFIELD

THE PENTAGONAL BUILDING in the centre had three doors with different addresses which must have caused some confusion for the postman. In 1888, it was occupied by the draper, Adam Greenhalgh, who ran his business from 23 Bury Road on the right of the property but lived at 2 Rochdale Road on the left. When this photograph was taken in 1911, Fred Dewhurst was running a plumbing business from there at 23 Market Place. On the front right of the picture, the confectioners and refreshment room was run by James Haworth for over thirty years and, in 1911, he was assisted by his wife Elizabeth. The inaugural meeting

of Edenfield Cricket Club was held on these premises in February 1902.

BLEAKHOLT ANIMAL SANCTUARY used the central shop to raise funds in the early 1960s but, by 1967, it was unoccupied and demolished in 1987 after much local debate; a low curved wall now represents the shape of the original structure. The Edenfield Residents Association used a line drawing of the building on their letterhead. Although the Edenfield bypass reduced traffic through the village, a zebra crossing is still required at this busy junction. These were first installed in the UK in 1951 with flashing Belisha beacons made from glass, but they were replaced with plastic the following year because children kept throwing stones at them! The zigzag road markings to prohibit parking were introduced in 1971. The confectioners has been replaced by a building behind the railings whose ground-floor offices were occupied by Stopford Construction (Rossendale) Ltd from the mid-1970s to 1998. A quality control company on the front left advertises 'Systems for Lean Manufacturing', which would not have been understood by the four butchers in Edenfield in 1909!

BURY ROAD, TOWNSENDFOLD

THIS VIEW WAS taken after September 1911, when the
Royal Pavilion Cinema opened on Bury Road in the centre
of Rawtenstall; there is a poster on the end of the low wall
on the right advertising its programme. Brookfield House
on the middle left was the home of Mary Ann Townsend, a
widow, and her two children, who were all described in 1911
as having private means. She sold land for £150 on which
Townsendfold Primitive Methodist Chapel in the far distance
was built. This 'neat but plain structure of stone' was built by
James Walton of Horncliffe Quarries at a cost of £800 and
opened on 6 February 1868 to seat a congregation of 300.
In 1912, the licensee of the Hare and Hounds on the middle
right was Robert Heyworth, whose son Sydney succeeded him
as landlord until 1970.

THE METHODIST CHAPEL closed for worship in November 1970 and was used as a
showroom for domestic appliances in the 1990s, but it is now divided into flats for let
and a variety of small businesses reflecting changes to our lifestyle. A tattoo studio
is used by both sexes as an increasingly popular fashion statement. A dance fitness
studio called DLNW (Dance Like No One's Watching) would not have been necessary at
the turn of the twentieth century when people worked long hours at more physically
demanding jobs and household tasks, whilst church dances were part of the social
calendar. The public house officially re-opened as the Whitchaff Inn in May 1971, so
named from a combination of the name of the landlord, Robert Whitworth, and that of
his wife, whose maiden name was Chaffer. The leisurely pace of horse-drawn transport
has disappeared and the area to the front right of the photograph is now used for a car
and van hire business.

TOWNSENDFOLD

THE HOLME, on the left of the picture, was the home of the influential Townsend family for 200 years over seven generations. A porch, added after this photograph was taken, contained a date stone engraved with 1681, but the stone had disappeared by 1920. The Townsends were owners of a considerable amount of land, a number of mills and several properties in Balladen and Haslingden. The Holme was a busy place in 1891 when it was occupied by Joshua Townsend who had been born there and was fifty-nine years of age. He was described in the census as a retired cotton spinner and lived with his wife Ann, four daughters, three sons, an aunt, cook, housemaid and Elizabeth Robinson, a widow with four

children. Joshua was typical of many of the local, wealthy mill owners who involved themselves in public duty. Although in poor health for many years before his death in 1896, he was the secretary of a relief committee during the cotton famine, was active on the Board of Guardians and a member of Rawtenstall Local Board until 1883.

THE FAMILY HOME was demolished in the 1960s and has been replaced by new bungalows with large gardens. The cottages to the right were formerly a block of back to back cottages which have been knocked through and modernised; the windows for the dwelling on the right are particularly different now. A footpath runs to the left of the cottages along the River Irwell and New Hall Hey Mill (see overleaf) can just be seen in the middle distance behind the cottages. Although it is not possible to distinguish this, it is interesting to note that the name Hardman Brothers has been engraved in the stonework at the top of the mill facing away from Rawtenstall but towards The Holme and the railway line approaching from the south.

NEW HALL HEY MILL, RAWTENSTALL

THIS PHOTOGRAPH WAS taken by James Hargreaves in 1949. The Hardman Brothers built this woollen mill in 1862, following a large fire which caused several deaths and destroyed the original building. Abraham Stott, the landlord of the Shepherds Inn on Haslingden Road, saved the lives of some female workers who were trapped on the top floor. Richard Williams, who designed many of the architecturally notable buildings in Rossendale, was commissioned to design the new mill and make it as fireproof as possible. He regarded it as one of his hardest jobs as the foundations of the chimney were partly rafted on quicksand. The building suffered unusual damage in 1884 when large hailstones broke 1,200 panes of glass and, as early as 1887, the company supplied gas to their mills and their employees' homes. A letterhead in 1928 advertised the company

as 'manufacturers of baizes and bayetas for the South American markets, also serges, cloths, tweeds, blankets etc. for the home market'.

THESE WORKERS' COTTAGES were demolished after 1962 and have been replaced by the car park for the Old Cobblers' Fayre & Square Inn. This photograph was taken at the end of September 2012 just after the inn had re-opened following a month's closure for refurbishments. A play area, the Wacky Warehouse, and a special food menu for children would not have been available at public houses in the 1940s. The architectural gems of the mill and its Italianate chimney were registered as Grade II listed buildings on 7 June 1971 and the chimney is one of the outstanding landmarks in Rossendale. Hardman Brothers and Company ran the weaving and finishing plant until May 1950, after which it was acquired by David Whitehead and Company Ltd. The mill is now known as the Hardmans Business Centre and provides offices to let.

ST MARY'S CHAMBERS, RAWTENSTALL

NEW HALL HEY HOUSE, on the left, with New Hall Hey Hall visible above the single-storey building on the right, *c.* 1919. The hall was reputed to have been built around 1600 by a Nuttall of Ramsbottom. The house was converted to an auxiliary hospital in 1915 with sixty-six beds and, when it closed in March 1919, 700 wounded soldiers had been nursed there. It was visited daily by Carrie Whitehead, a granddaughter of David Whitehead, who was to become the first female Mayor of Rawtenstall in 1935. The imposing building with its Corinthian columns in the middle distance is the United Methodist Chapel on Haslingden Road which opened on 18 June 1857. It was built by David and Peter Whitehead at a cost of

£6,000 to accommodate 1,000 people, following a rift with Longholme Methodist Church, but Peter did later express regret at establishing another rival church in such close proximity.

THE WESTERN END of the central traffic island now stands on the site of these attractive houses which were demolished in June 1967 to make way for the construction of the A682 Edenfield bypass. This opened on 9 July 1969 and now forms part of the link road between the M62 and M65. The dual carriageway which joins the M66 brought Rossendale within convenient travelling distance for commuters to Manchester, resulting in large-scale housing development throughout the borough. Amongst the trees behind the traffic lights, the Rawtenstall annexe of Accrington and Rossendale College was officially opened on 30 October 1956, but it did not last as long as New Hall Hey Hall as structural defects were found in the concrete in 1981. It was demolished in 2008 and the site is still awaiting redevelopment. The Methodist chapel, renamed St Mary's Chambers, was refurbished in 1999 and now caters for weddings, conferences and parties.

HASLINGDEN OLD ROAD, RAWTENSTALL

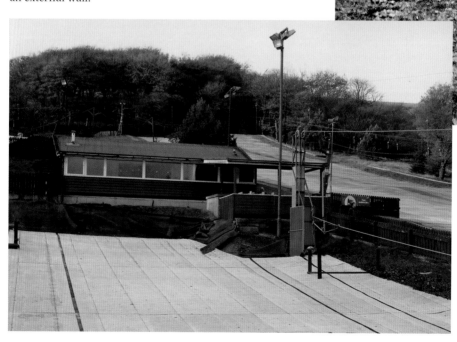

THE HIGHER PLAN cottages were built in 1687 in the area known as Oakenhead Wood. In February 1804, 22 acres were sold for £1,050 to William Cockerill of Haslingden who wished to invest money from his expanding business empire in Belgium. He had seen the advantages of exploiting his engineering skills by introducing the English inventions of wool-carding and wool-spinning machinery to the Continent, long before the concept of the European Union was formed. After he died in 1832, a small estate of 28 acres was sold for £2,500 on 23 March 1840 to George Hardman, who built Oak Hill as his family home overlooking his New Hall Hey Mill (see page thirty-six). The house in Whitaker Park is now occupied by Rossendale Museum which holds estate plans of Higher Plan and has a date stone from the cottages incorporated into an external wall.

A 'NEW LOCAL café with a plan', in the middle of the Rossendale Ski and Snowboard Centre, is now on the site with a practice area for beginners in the foreground. The cottages were demolished in the late 1960s and the ski slope was officially opened on 15 September 1973 by an Everest mountaineer, Sir Jack Longland, who announced that 'Rawtenstall is really making history. There is nothing like this in the whole of the north and it is the largest complex in England'. Although it was then an exciting and innovative leisure facility developed by a small borough council, recent cutbacks in local government spending led to its closure on 31 March 2011. It was taken over by a social enterprise organisation and celebrated its official re-opening later the same year on 5 November. The café boasts stunning views of the valley and is open to all, not just visitors to the ski slope.

RAWTENSTALL LIBRARY

HASLINGDEN ROAD, *c.* 1910. The new electric tramway had been officially opened on 15 May 1909. The 'new and magnificent' Grand Theatre was designed by Messrs Darbyshire and Smith, Manchester, to seat an audience of 2,000 people and it was built at a cost of £16,000. It opened on 31 July 1899 with a performance of Milton Rays' burlesque, *Don Quixote*, at a ticket price of 4*d* for a gallery seat. The public library on the right opened in 1906, funded by a grant from Andrew Carnegie 'to help those who help themselves'. Ambitious plans in 1903 for a magnificent Town Hall to be added to the library building were not realised and the brick gable wall anticipates this extension. The way the library is administered has changed considerably over the years; in August 1911, it was the decision of the chairman of the libraries committee and Councillor Brooks 'to obtain a suitable doormat for the entrance'!

THE ELECTRIC TRAM service ceased on 31 March 1932 to make way for the motor bus. Many other motor vehicles now use the petrol station standing on the site of St Mary's Parsonage and the *Rossendale Free Press* office. The local newspaper was based there from 1891 until its transfer to Bank Street in 1969. The theatre, renamed the Palace, was not a popular venue, with complaints that it was too large, cold and uncomfortable, and it was demolished over several months from October 1937. The bus station then operated here until it moved to its present location on Bacup Road in April 1967. Abortive plans for the large, new traffic island in the late 1960s included a prestigious new bus station and, in 1971, an area of water for paddling and sailing model boats was proposed! A fire station was built there instead behind the trees in 1989.

ST MARY'S WAY, RAWTENSTALL

THE ASTORIA BALLROOM provided unforgettable memories for music and dance lovers throughout the north west for thirty-three years from 16 December 1932 until its closure on 7 February 1966; there was then a loud chorus of complaints from 'disgusted' teenagers who had to travel out of town for their entertainment. The building was originally Holly Mount School, erected in 1839 by the Whitehead brothers for their employees' children. David wrote in his diary that 'there is real pleasure in spending a little money and doing good in this way'. It was later used as a car showroom and workshops by John Myerscough before conversion to a ballroom boasting one of the finest sprung dance floors in England. It could hold up to 800 dancers and played host to some of the biggest names on the music scene from the Ted Heath Orchestra and Cleo Laine to the Moody Blues and The Who.

THE ASTORIA WAS demolished in 1968 for the construction of the new road taking traffic from the Edenfield bypass northwards. Rawtenstall Civic Society campaigned for the creation of the Old Fold Garden which now occupies the site. The original date stone from the school has been mounted on the school clock tower and a modern date stone added to mark the opening of the garden by the Mayor, Councillor W.H. Nuttall, on 12 May 1979. Above the garden can be seen Holly Mount, the home of the Whitehead brothers who began building it in 1834. They cast lots to decide which one of the three houses they were each going to occupy, but all were 'well satisfied with his own lot'. The building is now under renovation as private apartments. Asda on the right opened on 14 August 2006 on the site of David Whitehead's Lower Mill.

BANK STREET, RAWTENSTALL

CANOPIES PROTECT FRESH produce around 1919 when buying food was much more a daily activity than today; there is now only one greengrocer on Bank Street. A funeral cortège in the distance leaves evidence of its horse-drawn transport on the road. When this photograph was donated to Rawtenstall Library in 1949, it was stated that 'not much change has taken place generally'. This was certainly not true two decades later with the closure of thirty shops and 120 residents displaced from their homes following the decision to build St Mary's Way. All the property on the left up to the current NatWest Bank with the dome has disappeared, except for the Ladbrokes premises which are just to the left of the modern photograph below. The two rows of shops on the middle right were also lost for the construction of a pedestrianised shopping precinct whose appearance attracted harsh criticism over the years. However, the council had felt, in 1962, that they had to redesign the town centre or 'the town will die'.

A BUSY CAR PARK and mature trees are now situated in front of the three-storey shops with their distinctive roof line, pictured above, so it has, therefore, not been possible to show their extensively altered façade. The two shops on the left of the row have been replaced by a building with an interesting first-floor balustrade, originally occupied by the Midland Bank but which was taken over by HSBC in 1999. On Saturday, 6 October 2012, a crowd of onlookers in the centre of the picture awaits the official opening of a town square, created on the site of the recently demolished Valley Centre. The 'new' Astoria ballroom had opened on the North Street side of the shopping centre on 25 October 1968, but memories of exciting times at the 'old' Astoria (see page forty-four) have been preserved in four specially commissioned mosaics, incorporated into a seating area on the corner of this public open space beyond the crowd. Rawtenstall Annual Fair continued the day's celebrations with music and dancing demonstrations entertaining many visitors in 'a new beginning for the town'.

KAY STREET BAPTIST CHURCH, RAWTENSTALL

THE ORIGINAL SCHOOL-CHAPEL before 1901. In 1871, the Revd John Jefferson began preaching in the Holly Mount school room and, by the following year, had created a new church with eighteen members. A fundraising concert, where electric lights were used,

attracted crowds looking on in amazement at this new type of light, but the supply failed and one of the party complained, 'We want no moor blue leet'. James Walton succeeded in building the chapel, which opened on 21 December 1876, as 'one of the few completed at a cost under rather than over'. Richard Whitaker had donated £1,000 and his wife, who was very involved in the work of the church, was remembered as 'a fragrance and an inspiration'.

ORIGINAL PLANS TO build a separate church were not realised until 20 April 1901 when foundation stones were laid by Mrs Richard Whitaker of St Annes on the Sea; R.H. Crabtree of Southport; Alderman D. Greenwood, JP of Bacup; and Alderman H.W. Trickett, JP, Mayor of Rawtenstall. Memorial stones were laid to the founder of the church by his son, William Jefferson, and to John Heyworth, deacon and treasurer, by his widow. The church officially opened on 10 September 1902. Services are now held on the first floor, with the ground floor accessible for community events, and the original chapel just visible to the rear is used as the Sunday school and church hall. On the left of the picture is the property listed as the police headquarters in the council yearbooks from 1894 to 1950. The maxim of the first Chief Constable of Lancashire in 1839, that constables should 'be cool and intrepid in the discharge of duties', has an ironical twist now the building is an Indian restaurant! Photographs of the town centre before its 1960s redevelopment are displayed on the wall of the police station garage.

BACUP ROAD, RAWTENSTALL

A PHOTOGRAPH OF the Town Hall, taken by H. Sykes, *c.* 1905. This opened in 1875 as a share exchange with rooms for conversation, smoking and refreshments where business could be transacted in surroundings more salubrious than a public house. It was 'fitted with every modern improvement regardless of cost... to compare with any first-class hotel'. Rawtenstall became a Local Board on 6 August 1874, but its officials wished to improve the status of the area in 1887 by securing a charter of incorporation as a borough. This was at first refused because of Rawtenstall's size – at the time it was the largest Local Board District in the country. These premises were acquired as temporary municipal offices in 1890 when it was certain that Rawtenstall would be granted borough status on 2 February 1891. When plans to build a Town Hall and Assembly Rooms next to the library foundered, this building was retained. The canvas tent is part of Rawtenstall Fair which 'used to be a marvellous fair – with coconut stalls and roundabouts'.

THE LOCAL COUNCIL soon realised their municipal offices were too small and a tender to extend the building in the same architectural style was accepted in December 1910 from Ormerod Ashworth, who had also won the contract for the masonry and joinery work on Kay Street Baptist Church in 1901. The shape of the former doorway can be seen in the stonework. The site of the fair is now occupied by the bus station which moved here initially as a temporary measure only. The white police station opened with many modern facilities on 13 May 1974. It was built on the site of Jubilee Primitive Methodist Church, on the edge of the original photograph, which had closed on 3 October 1965 after 104 years of worship.

WEAVERS' COTTAGE, FALLBARN ROAD, RAWTENSTALL

ILEX LEVEL CROSSING before the last diesel train ran from Rawtenstall to Bacup on
3 December 1966, arriving shortly after midnight. The railway line from Salford to
Rawtenstall opened in 1846 when 12,279 tickets were booked in the first six days.
The single line from Rawtenstall was extended across this bridge over the River Irwell

to Newchurch on 27 March 1848, but the pressure of increasing traffic led the company to double the line; this new line opened on 4 July 1880. The signal box to the left of the picture was unique because it was built into the river bed. Travelling by train was a little exhausting then – in 1858 a holiday excursion was offered from Rawtenstall to Harrogate, setting off at 10 a.m. but only arriving in Harrogate twelve hours later!

THE WEAVERS' COTTAGE was built as one unit to house looms in the 1780s. It is one of the finest surviving examples of an eighteenth-century loomshop and one of the oldest buildings in Rossendale. It was saved from demolition after a listing of historical importance in 1970 when Rawtenstall Civic Society bought and carefully restored it as its headquarters and a heritage centre. It is now an important visitor attraction with working hand looms, a Victorian kitchen, clog shop and tea room. The railway line has been replaced by Bocholt Way, bypassing the town centre. Behind the trees on the left is the car park for Ilex Mill, built by Peter Whitehead in 1856 and designated a Grade II listed building in 1982. It has been restored as private apartments. Rossendale Primary Health Care Centre on the right has been built on the site of the cotton mill, Albion Mill, and was officially opened by the High Sheriff of Lancashire on 18 November 2010.

BURNLEY ROAD, CRAWSHAWBOOTH

THESE STREET DECORATIONS have been laid out to celebrate Queen Victoria's Diamond Jubilee in June 1897. The Manchester and County Bank (see overleaf) in the far distance has since been demolished along with the building in front of it protruding into the road. The steam tramway, run by the Rossendale Valley Steam Tramways Company, opened from Rawtenstall on 12 September 1891 and passengers could shelter in a waiting room in the Friendship Inn which can be seen on the front left. Weekly takings for the inn were £24 in

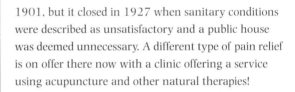

1901, but it closed in 1927 when sanitary conditions were described as unsatisfactory and a public house was deemed unnecessary. A different type of pain relief is on offer there now with a clinic offering a service using acupuncture and other natural therapies!

THIS PHOTOGRAPH WAS taken on Monday, 4 June 2012 when the country was enjoying a double Bank Holiday to celebrate the Diamond Jubilee of Queen Elizabeth II. The road is now a well-used thoroughfare from Rawtenstall to Burnley, so cannot be decorated in the elaborate style of 1897 or used for social events. There are a couple of Union Jacks over the shops on the left and the gardens on the right have been decorated, but there is only a small flag visible in the tree on the edge of the pavement. These gardens were improved by a local environment group to celebrate the Queen's Golden Jubilee in 2002. The village did mark the Diamond Jubilee in style on Tuesday 5 June, away from the busy main road, at Rakefoot Wesleyan Methodist Church hall on York Street. There were performances from the Valley Academy's School of Musical Theatre and Dance and the Valley Aloud Community Choir, with a variety of refreshments provided by an outdoor bar, a barbecue and afternoon teas.

CO-OPERATION STREET, CRAWSHAWBOOTH

THE MANCHESTER AND County Bank in 1911. Notices in the windows direct customers to premises 'across the road' during its temporary closure. The upper floor of the bank was occupied by a solicitors, John Sutcliffe and Sons. The bank and Crawshaw's shop beyond, which has almost disappeared, were both demolished in a road-widening scheme. This removed a sharp S-bend where the trams often left the tram lines. On 9 August 1924, an intermittent bus service began running from Rawtenstall to Burnley Summit, but a regular timetable could not be implemented because there were not enough drivers; a full service did not commence until

April 1932. Mansion House Buildings is the row of shops whose gable end faces the camera and which can just be seen on the modern photograph.

THE NEW BANK was designed well to take advantage of its corner location and a date stone for 1913 has been incorporated below the chimney on the Burnley Road elevation. The bank manager used to live on the first floor and this accommodation is now rented out as a flat. The bank merged with the District Bank in 1935, but this was taken over in turn by National Westminster Bank in 1970. The building closed as a bank in March 1983 and was purchased by Eric Ingham and Company who continued the financial work of the premises with an accountancy service still in operation today. The Halifax Building Society rented space in the property to run a small branch for around five years in the late 1980s. The windows have been replaced on the ground floor, but the interior of the building has not been altered. The initials of the original bank, MC, are still etched in the glass panels of internal doors and the original wood panelling, bank counter and screen complete with bell have all survived.

THE BLACK DOG, CRAWSHAWBOOTH

THIS INN, PICTURED around 1906, was open on Mondays, Wednesdays and Saturdays in 1842 for the stagecoach service from Burnley to Manchester and, later, in the 1870s the Wint family ran a horse-bus from here to Burnley. Isaac Wint was a resourceful fellow and also sold meat in the butcher's shop which can be seen at the front left of the building. Isaac was the landlord for forty-six years and, when he retired in 1926, it ended a family

association of over sixty years. This building was demolished in 1933 and replaced in 1936 by the premises shown above, although they were set further back from the road. The roof of Rakefoot Wesleyan Methodist Church can be seen to the right. It opened on 8 September 1867 and, in 1869, was described as 'one of the handsomest structures in this part of the country'. The church could originally seat a congregation of 1,040, but closed its doors in 1980 with services now being held in the Sunday school to the rear. The church has recently been renovated as private apartments.

THE ROAD THROUGH Crawshawbooth is lined with adults and children in party mood on Saturday, 23 June 2012, probably the only day the car park in front of this public house will ever be occupied by people rather than cars and vans! The car park had been designated as a viewing point for the crowds, who are out with their Union Jacks, waiting to welcome the Olympic Flame on its seventy-day journey across the UK, celebrating the London 2012 Olympic Games. The previous day had seen a month's rainfall in twenty-four hours causing severe flooding both in Crawshawbooth and throughout the north west, but extensive efforts had been made to clean the centre of the village for this special day.

610 BURNLEY ROAD, CRAWSHAWBOOTH

A. CANE, CABINET maker and house furnisher, *c.* 1900. This long-established business traded from 1883 to 1967 and was available 'for the making of chairs, tables and bedsteads'. In 1950, the services were advertised as 'complete house furnishers' selling 'reliable utility furniture'. The grandson, Arthur, opened a similar shop on Newchurch Road in Rawtenstall and many couples remembered setting up home 'with Cane's just like Mum and Dad'. The last section of new steam tramway in Britain ran in front of this shop in

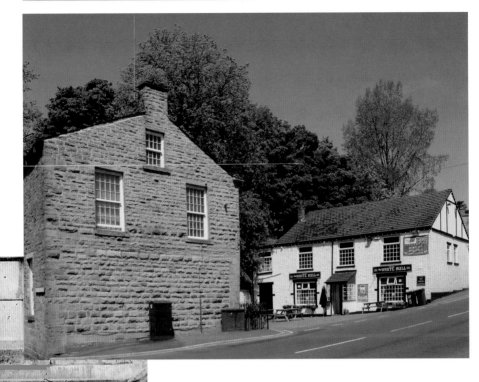

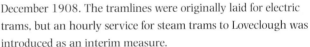

December 1908. The tramlines were originally laid for electric trams, but an hourly service for steam trams to Loveclough was introduced as an interim measure.

A CLOSE LOOK at the gable wall of this building on the corner of Barley Holme Road will reveal the shape of the frontage of the furniture shop. A more prominent horizontal row of stonework indicates where the sign advertised the shop's activities and a small telephone junction box marks the location of the door. The windows above the stonework can be seen in the same place on both photographs but the window frames have been modernised. After the shop closed, it was occupied from 1981 to 1988 by Ram Services Ltd who were structural repair specialists and are now located in Burnley. The premises were eventually bought in 2001 and have been converted into two private dwellings. The White Bull was serving drinks in 1818 when the licensee was Anne Bentley and it was later used as a waiting room for the horse-bus to Burnley. It was damaged by fire in 1980 but was rebuilt to re-open a decade later and is still serving drinks as a traditional English pub. The Indian restaurant now operating from the first floor offers a menu which would have seemed strange to Mr Cane.

BURNLEY ROAD, LOVECLOUGH

CHARLES ED. DEAN at Loveclough Industrial Co-operative Society, 928 Burnley Road, *c.* 1920. This shop opened in the early 1880s on its corner site with windows on two sides to attract more customers. It joined many others in Rossendale established as self-help organisations to promote independence, encourage savings and improve living standards. The larger stores also acted as community centres and the Crawshawbooth society, which traded from 1864, also had a meeting hall for 400 people and a library

with over 100 volumes. The co-operative movement 'kept poverty from many a working man's door', according to Thomas Newbigging, who wrote *History of the Forest of Rossendale*.

THIS BUILDING HAS retained a commercial purpose, providing a printing and stationery service which has operated from this location since 1967. The original pigeonhole shelving, work top and meat hook have survived inside the room under the sign. The stonework around the window on Burnley Road indicates the outline of the vertical sides of the original ornate window surround. Additional stone courses under the window have enabled a smaller window frame to be inserted. The lintel above the doorway with a small circle engraved in the centre is the same and this design can be seen in all the houses on the row from Nos 914 to 928. On the gable wall, the stonework around the first-floor left-hand window shows the shape of a doorway where a projecting steel beam for a hoist would have lifted goods to the first-floor storage area – this feature would also have been incorporated into other co-operative society buildings. The 30mph speed limit was not in force in Charles's day. A speed limit of 20mph had been introduced in 1903, but it was 1934 when a 30mph limit was enforced for roads in built-up areas.

LOVECLOUGH FOLD

LOVECLOUGH MANSION HOUSE. A date stone from a fireplace inside the house inscribed with 'R.H. 1741' probably refers to an ancestor of Richard Holt who owned Loveclough Printworks in 1832. The Rossendale Printing Company was operating the mill in 1870 when it came into the ownership of the cotton spinner and merchant Joseph Cocksey Lee, who was knighted in 1882. The company acquired the Mansion House to provide accommodation for him on his visits from his home in Dunham Massey near Altrincham. It became a club house for the printworkers in 1897 with a bar and games room on the ground floor, library and reading room upstairs and a bowling green at the rear. Following Joseph's death in 1894, his eldest son, Lennox Bertram, took the company into the Calico Printers' Association in 1899 and the amalgamation brought

together forty-six printing firms and thirteen merchants to form what was then the United Kingdom's largest company.

THIS PEACEFUL RETREAT has survived as the C.P.A. Social and Bowling Club, with an active membership of around 250 still enjoying the facilities of snooker, a bowling green and rooms to hire for parties. The club and the two adjacent barns, now converted into private homes, are in a designated conservation area as 'a rare survivor of a pre-industrial agricultural settlement'. Modern housing has been built to the left of the picture on the site of Loveclough Printworks (which closed in July 1980). When Tootal announced its closure with a loss of 240 jobs, increasing imports and reduced consumer spending were blamed. There are some magnificent large photographs of the printworks in the clubhouse. Satellite television has recently been installed bringing a much wider variety of sports to the members than was available in the 1890s!

NEWCHURCH ROAD, HIGHER CLOUGHFOLD

LODGE FOLD FARM was built in 1629 by the Revd William Horrocks who was curate of St Nicholas's Parish Church from 1622 until his death in 1641 and it was inhabited as a rectory until 1850. Higher Cloughfold also became an important meeting place for

Nonconformists from the late 1600s to the early 1700s and Sion Baptist Church, overleaf, grew out of this movement. The barn on the left of the picture was rebuilt in 1854 and, in the late 1920s, was used to store bonfire wood. This was safe from raiding 'bonfire gangs' because a female resident in one of the cottages would chase them away!

THE FARM WAS demolished in the mid-1930s and the garden area now allows a safer view around the sharp bend opposite the Red Lion public house. Higher Cloughfold has been designated a conservation area since March 1975 with a wide variety of building styles dating from 1700 onwards, some of which reflect the early development of the textile industry. The gable end on the right-hand side of Newchurch Road belongs to Ashworth Buildings, built around 1840 as back to back dwellings for handloom weavers, but they were converted to larger houses in 1977. The cottage behind the tree on the old photograph was demolished sometime between 1891 and 1908. On the left of the modern picture can now be seen the chimney stack of Springhill House. In 1896 this home was advertised for let as a 'commodious family residence with 35-40 acres of superior grass land' and supplied with 'pure spring water'. Seconds after this photograph was taken, a large deer ran across the road from the right and jumped into one of the gardens to the left of the picture.

SION BAPTIST CHURCH, HIGHER CLOUGHFOLD

SION BAPTIST CHURCH was founded around 1672 and, on 11 February 1705, Robert
Litchford made a deed to give his home to the local Baptists as a place of worship.
The church, pictured here after 1902, was built in 1839 and enlarged in 1854. The
Sunday school, to the right of the church and beyond the graveyard, had fourteen
foundation stones laid on 15 June 1901; this is the largest number on any building in

Rossendale and includes one laid by Richard Whitaker, who donated Rossendale Museum and its park to the people of Rawtenstall in 1901. The Sunday school also boasts the longest date stone in the borough – engraved with 'Sion Baptist Sunday School, Cloughfold, AD 1901'.

THE CONGREGATION TRANSFERRED to the Sunday school building with arched windows on the right in October 1984 before the church was demolished to make way for the Litchford House flats which were built in 1986. At the last wedding in the church before its demolition, there was no electricity supply so the electric blower for the organ did not work. However, the organ could still be used to celebrate the couple's special day as the hand pump was operated by the organist's son. The gable end of the flats sympathetically echoes the roof line of the original church and some features from the old building were re-used in the new flats. The gateposts are the same but the gates have disappeared. The recycling bins on the pavement reflect the environmental pressures there have been over recent years, where local authorities are trying to reduce the amount of waste material which goes to landfill. Of course, people at the turn of twentieth century recycled in a much more efficient way by taking bottles and containers to shops to be re-filled.

BURNLEY ROAD EAST, WATER

LOOKING NORTH ON a traffic-free road around 1900, the lane leading to the village of Dean is on the right, next to the building now called the Water Village Store. This area is of national significance because of the Deighn Layrocks, or the Larks of Dean, a band of musicians performing between 1740 and the 1860s. They were textile, agricultural or quarry workers by day but composers, musicians and singers by night. They would have walked along this road and the moorland paths between their homes and Goodshaw Old Baptist Chapel to play both sacred and secular music, often into the early hours of the morning. They composed many of their own hymn tunes and some of their instruments and manuscript songbooks can be viewed in Rossendale Museum.

PEDESTRIANS HAVE GIVEN way to the motor vehicle, but the bus passengers have a smoother ride on the tarmac road surface than those travelling on Rawtenstall's first motor bus service between Waterfoot and Water in 1907. Although the road surface on the left does not appear too rough, there were many complaints that the buses jolted passengers 'almost to insensibility' and pedestrians were splashed with mud in wet weather or almost suffocated by dust clouds in dry conditions. The service was so unreliable that it was replaced by electric trams in 1911 until 31 March 1931 when buses took over for a second and final time. The small trailer on the left belongs to a car valeting service – an unaffordable luxury for the worker on the original photograph who would have had to clean his cart himself. The green car displays the business mobile phone number. This very new technology was only introduced into the UK in 1985 but has revolutionised the way we communicate, a century after the first use of a telephone in the area.

STACKSTEADS RAILWAY STATION, NEAR BLACKWOOD ROAD

THE LINE THROUGH Stacksteads from Rawtenstall to Bacup had been opened on 1 October 1852 but, in January 1853, a letter to the *Manchester Examiner and Times* complained that there was no 'room of any sort to take shelter from the piercing cold and when ... trains are invariably behind time I ... think such a convenience ought to be provided'. That passenger would certainly have been pleased in May 1856 when tenders were awarded for waiting rooms to be built at Stacksteads. Increasing traffic led to the decision in 1876 to extend the single line to a double and a new island platform, station and subway were made available for public viewing at a gala on Sunday, 15 August 1880. The *Bacup Times* reported that 'people were a little puzzled. There was a decided inclination for them to lose themselves by rushing over the level crossing instead of diving down the subway; visitors also rambled on to the temporary wooden platform instead of the brand new American-looking one just completed.'

THE STATION WAS demolished after the line closed to all traffic on 3 December 1966 following the Beeching cuts. This bridge housing the island platform had been one of six river crossings over the River Irwell within three quarters of a mile before the Bacup tunnel. As can be seen from this view taken from Blackwood Bridge looking towards Siding Street, the bridge is now fenced off and disused. The car park for new housing, Blackwood Mews, is to the right of the retaining wall. Several private sidings used by local companies to transport goods to and from their premises, some of which were also served by narrow-gauge tracks to carry stone from the local quarries, have also disappeared and been replaced by other industrial development along the course of the railway line.

MARKET STREET, BACUP

TRAM TRACKS CAN be seen for a service which officially
opened on 3 August 1889. Shopkeepers on Market Street
complained about a loss in trade as some of their customers
now caught the steam tram to the railway station instead of
walking past their shops. The terminus was intended to be
the Bull's Head Hotel in the middle distance, but the steam
engine often left the rails on turning up Burnley Road so it
was changed to the Market Hotel. Electric trams replaced
'the horrid smell and smoking' of the steam trams when
the last one used for a regular service in Britain operated in
Bacup on 22 July 1909.

THE BULL'S HEAD Hotel was demolished by Glen Top
Brewery in 1911 and replaced by the King George V
public house with the clock tower. It opened on
6 December 1912 and, when King George V and Queen
Mary visited Lancashire the following year, it was the
only hostelry in the country to bear the name of the

reigning monarch. In 1936, the landlord, Horace Aldren, was growing mushrooms in the cellar! The public house closed in 1983 and has been renamed the King George Chambers, occupied by a variety of companies, including an advertising and website design business; any organisation without a website now is at a serious disadvantage in the modern market place. Many alterations have been made to the façade of the shops on the left, one of which offers a luxury service of eyelash extensions. By comparison, in 1909, when money had to be spent on more essential items, Market Street had eleven grocers, eight butchers, two chimney sweeps and an artificial teeth manufacturer! The more ornate shop to the front left was built with dressed stone in 1921, later than the rest of the row.

BURNLEY ROAD, BACUP

THE WONDER OF the combustion engine almost meets its match in the snows of Bacup in the late 1930s. The programme for the Festival of Britain celebrations of 1951 highlighted the delights of local climatic conditions when it described a gentleman arriving at the railway station and asking a small boy, 'Does it always rain in Bacup?' The boy replied, 'Oh no, it snows sometimes!' The white building on the right was designed by a Bacup architect, Harry Cropper, and opened as the New Regal Cinema on the afternoon of 7 September 1931. A new wonder 'expanding screen' was the first in east Lancashire. An advertisement encouraged cinema-goers to 'Come to Brighter Bacup to see the Regal. The last word in entertainment luxury.'

WATERSIDE UNITED METHODIST Free Church on the left was built in 1897, but was renamed Central Methodist Church in 1952. The railings opposite enclose the Blind Garden which has a plaque for No. 5 on the Bacup Trail; the Britannia Coconut Dancers pass here every Easter Saturday performing their traditional folk dances from Britannia through the centre of Bacup to Stacksteads, wearing out a set of clog irons in the process. When this photograph was taken, the shop on the front right offered a website design service, an unknown technology even in the 1930s, reflecting the rapid pace of change over just eighty years. The former cinema on the right closed on 29 June 1968 to become the New Embassy Bingo Club which closed around 1996. The building was bought by a Middle Eastern businessman in 2005 for redevelopment, but diverse plans to renovate the building for leisure, business or retail purposes, as proposed by Bacup residents, have not borne fruit and the building remains derelict, although now owned by local entrepreneur Brian Boys.

AGED, BLIND AND DISABLED CENTRE, BACUP

WAITING FOR A horse on an outing from the Liberal Club. This building was formally opened on 18 March 1893 by John Henry Maden of Rockliffe House, following a procession from the original club on Rochdale Road. The architects, Messrs Mangnall and Littlewoods, Manchester, also designed the Maden Public Baths in Bacup and the Winter Gardens Empress Ballroom in Blackpool. The club boasted two billiards rooms, a lecture room to hold an audience of 500 and a reference library and reading room where concentration

was aided by the ruling that no intoxicating liquors were to be sold on the premises. A World's Fair fundraising bazaar with conjuring, ventriloquist and musical entertainment was held in the club on 19 October 1892. The handbook urged visitors to 'Buy, buy, buy, and when you have bought bye, bye!' and ordered that, 'Grumbling, fault-finding and offence-taking are strictly forbidden'.

BETTER LATE THAN never! Horses are used more now for leisure purposes than for essential transport. Four foundation stones, two of which can be seen on the right of this impressive front façade, were dedicated to J.H. Maden MP, Aldermen D. Greenwood and Disley, and James Shepherd, who had all given generous donations to the club. There was, however, still a debt of £441 when it opened – so current financial troubles are nothing new! The building was refurbished in 1966 as part of an improvement programme to make the town centre more attractive and was officially opened as the 'truly magnificent' Aged, Blind and Disabled Centre on 10 December by the Mayor, Councillor J. Kershaw. He remembered being taught how to play billiards in the Liberal Club in his youth, but praised the modern additions of a television room and telephone. Groups meeting there now include slimming, karate, snooker and lunchtime clubs.

YORKSHIRE STREET, BACUP

FOUR LICENSED PREMISES can be seen on this short stretch of road which could explain the presence of a policeman on duty on the middle left of the picture. The Queens Hotel at the front left was built with stabling for five horses and a coach house. Further along at No. 22 with the white boards above the first floor is The White Horse Inn. Next door is the Hare and Hounds Inn, built originally as two cottages in 1804, and, on the opposite side of the road, is The Green Man Hotel, which closed on 30 September 1924 after its licence was refused as unnecessary. However, this pub had been poorly maintained for some time, with

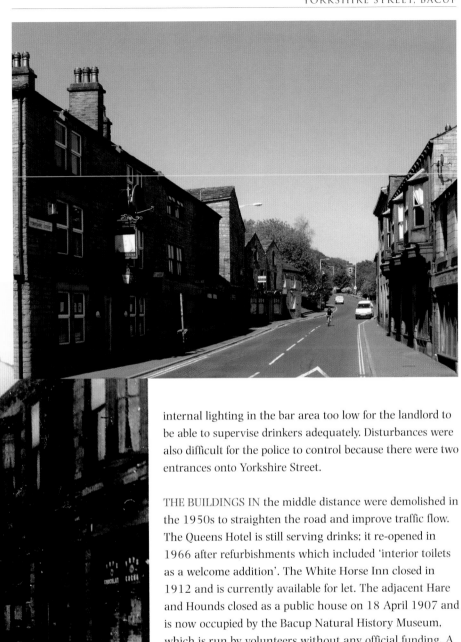

internal lighting in the bar area too low for the landlord to be able to supervise drinkers adequately. Disturbances were also difficult for the police to control because there were two entrances onto Yorkshire Street.

THE BUILDINGS IN the middle distance were demolished in the 1950s to straighten the road and improve traffic flow. The Queens Hotel is still serving drinks; it re-opened in 1966 after refurbishments which included 'interior toilets as a welcome addition'. The White Horse Inn closed in 1912 and is currently available for let. The adjacent Hare and Hounds closed as a public house on 18 April 1907 and is now occupied by the Bacup Natural History Museum, which is run by volunteers without any official funding. A fascinating variety of objects illustrates the natural history, geology, industry, religion and social aspects of Bacup's history and there is a regular programme of evening lectures. Across the road at No. 15, the three-storey Green Man Hotel has been turned into private accommodation. A pizza and kebab shop at the front right would have puzzled the local drinkers at the turn of the twentieth century!

ST JAMES'S SQUARE, BACUP

BOOTS CASH CHEMISTS (Lancashire) Ltd, *c.* 1935. This shop will soon be celebrating a centenary in the same premises. It opened in what was then 15 Bridge Street on 16 January 1914, one of 550 stores throughout England, Scotland and Wales. A successful business had developed from a small herbalist store, established in Nottingham in 1849 by John Boot, an agricultural worker. His herbal remedies soon proved popular, especially with the working poor, who could not afford the services of a doctor. It is ironical to note that, in 2012, we are now being encouraged to use our local pharmacist as a surrogate doctor for minor ailments. The style of shop displays has obviously changed now to a less cluttered

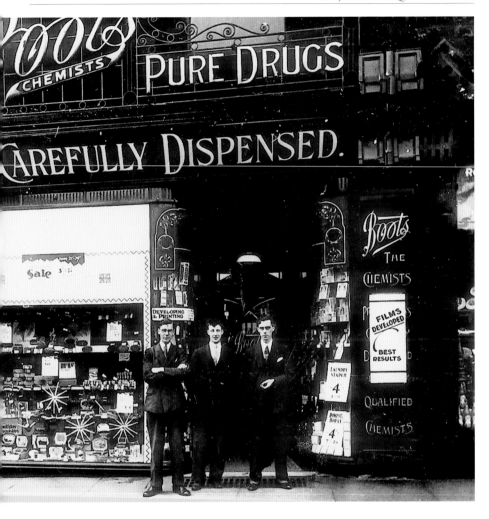

format, but the poster on the right advertising 'films developed' highlights recent changes in the way we take photographs using digital cameras and mobile phones.

THERE HAVE BEEN many developments in front of this shop on the site of the traffic island. The property, known as Townhead, which included the George and Dragon Inn, was demolished in 1927 to ease traffic congestion and replaced firstly by an open cobbled square and then, in 1952, with a roundabout. Interesting detail can be seen on the upper storeys of the shop premises; a wide range of elaborate architectural features can be seen on buildings throughout Rossendale, but they are normally missed on shopping trips. Although Bacup has its fair share of empty and disused buildings, it has not suffered the draconian changes that wholesale demolitions of the 1960s brought to other Lancashire towns and Bacup town centre was designated a conservation area in 1981, with English Heritage proclaiming it the 'best preserved cotton town in England'. The Union Jacks are marking Diamond Jubilee celebrations for Queen Elizabeth II.

BACUP LIBRARY

FIRST WORLD WAR recruitment campaign outside the Mechanics' Institute, *c.* 1914-1915. When war was declared on 4 August 1914, the army was manned by volunteers and conscription was only introduced later on 27 January 1916. Five thousand men from Bacup served in the war. The Mechanics' Institute opened in 1846 with the town's first library, reading room and museum. The premises were also used as a non-denominational day school, which was unique at the time when all other schools were church related. The institute's chief purpose was to educate working people, but leisure time was also important and a concert in 1871 promised 'two hours of refined mirth and song'. The building had been taken over by Bacup Corporation in January 1909 and the large Assembly Hall on the first floor was used for public concerts and functions.

THREE WOODEN TABLETS in the Aged, Blind and Disabled Centre (see page seventy-nine)
commemorate the 515 men who died in the war; another tablet was added later to
honour 140 lost in the Second World War. Trooper Wilfred Birch, who lost his sight
during the war, unveiled a war memorial on Burnley Road on 10 November 1928
in 'ceaseless, drenching rain'. The ground floor of the Mechanics' Institute became
the public library on 27 June 1931 with almost 1,000 books transferred from the
first-floor library of the Co-operative Society on Rochdale Road, shown overleaf. A
wide-ranging local history collection was developed with newspapers from 1863 and
nineteenth-century census returns on microfilm. Administration of the library transferred
to Lancashire County Council at local government re-organisation in 1974 since when
the service has been much changed due to the influence of the internet, with computers
available free for public use. Bacup Judo Club has occupied the upper floor since 1980.

BACUP CO-OPERATIVE STORE, ROCHDALE ROAD

THE TEA PARTY for 2,000 members to celebrate the official opening on Good Friday, 3 April 1863 'was the greatest social gathering there had been in Bacup'. A meeting of seven individuals in a garret in 1847 resulted in what became the largest co-operative society in Rossendale. A date stone inscribed with 'Bacup Co-operative Store Limited 1862' is on display in the Wall of History on Yorkshire Street. The name 'Bacup' was

covered up during the Second World War to confuse the Germans if they arrived in town! At one time this shop contained all departments except footwear, including a bakery, slaughterhouse, library and large concert room. The poster in the window is publicising the opening on 27 June 1914 of the furnishing and tailoring departments in the new co-operative building with a clock tower, now renamed Pioneer Buildings, and shown above.

THE ORIGINAL CO-OP building was demolished in October 1977 and has been replaced by a council car park behind the low hedge along the pavement. The name of Pioneer Buildings recalls the achievements of the co-operative movement established by the Rochdale Equitable Pioneers Society in 1844 with the aim of alleviating poverty. One of their rules was to manufacture articles to create employment for those 'suffering in consequence of repeated reductions in their wages'. The commercial purpose of the building has continued with sales of sweets, gifts, children's clothing, carpets and refreshments. On the first floor is a dance academy and the new home of Bacup Conservative Club, which unveiled its premises in March 2011. The public baths, just visible on the right of the original photograph, re-opened in July 2004 as the Maden Community and Children's Centre, part of a government-funded initiative. The Sure Start centre offers support services for parents with young children which, in 1914, would only have been provided by extended family and neighbours.

ROCHDALE ROAD, BACUP

AN EXPECTANT CROWD is gathered outside No. 174 Rochdale Road waiting for a procession from Thorn Wesleyan Methodist Chapel. When this church opened on Alma Street on Sunday, 5 May 1872, the collection raised amounted to a very generous £135. The congregation had previously met in a school-chapel on Union Street, which was known locally as the 'Chapel for the Destitute' or, more commonly, as 'Bacup Ragged School'. Most of the ladies are wearing hats and, in 1913, there were as many as eight milliners in Bacup. The female life expectancy at this time was only around fifty-five years of age with infections causing 63 per cent of all premature deaths between 1911 and 1915. Only 5 per cent of the population was aged over sixty-five between 1851 and 1911 when care and support for the elderly were provided by families, the Church and, *in extremis*, the workhouse.

THIS TERRACED ROW was demolished sometime after 1967 and the site is now occupied by Barker Court Housing 21, whose first residents moved in around 1982. The occupants of these one-bedroom flats, who must be over fifty-five, benefit from the presence of a resident manager, communal facilities and an active social programme. Improved living conditions, sanitation and hygiene have resulted in a marked increase in the elderly population so, by 2011, one in six of the population was over sixty-five. The speed camera on the middle left of the photograph reflects the modern necessity for greater control of speeding traffic – this would have been less of a problem with horse-drawn vehicles or even trams. This new technology was only introduced after the Road Traffic Act 1991 ruled that evidence from the cameras could be used to prove an offence had been committed.

MARKET STREET, FACIT

RATEPAYERS IN 1874 voted by 1,069 to 554 for the formation of a Local Board which operated from the first floor of No. 741 Market Street until Whitworth Urban District Council was established twenty years later. 'Board Room' can faintly be seen engraved on the window on the right with 'Surveyors Office' on the left. The ground floor was occupied by a grocer's shop whose goods can be seen on display; the shop was run in 1891 by Sarah Grindrod, a widow with three children. In 1879, there was news of 'a novel character' when workers in the Whitworth Local Board District responded to

cuts in wages and working hours by refusing to buy coal, milk, butter and even gas. This was a successful ploy and reductions were made to cottage rents and the prices of some grocery and drapery goods. At the first meeting of the Urban District Council, the first chairman, William Ernest Whitworth, stated that 'Whitworth is generally spoken of as a decaying village but this is a mistaken impression'.

A BAKERY SHOP has occupied this building for many years. The present owner of the property ran the shop from 1966 to 1989 and also converted the first-floor offices to a flat in 1973/4; the ginnel to the right of the door was filled in at the same time. The address of the former Local Board office should actually be Spring Place because access is through the rear of the building and not through the shop. The terraced row to the right was demolished in the late 1970s. In March 2012, the shop was used not only by passing trade on a busy road but also by workmen who were demolishing the nearby Facit Mill, built in 1904–05 as a fireproof ring spinning mill.

CHEETHAM HILL, FACIT

BACK TO BACK houses on Cheetham Hill around 1910 lay in the shadow of Facit Mill, which provided much vital work for these families. The railway line from Rochdale to Bacup was also essential to local employment, but one of the residents of this small community, Esther Smith, a thirty-six-year-old weaver, lost her life in what was the most serious accident to occur on the line. On Saturday, 29 August 1891, a goods train with twenty-four trucks, carrying stone from Britannia, ran into the rear of a passenger train at Facit; the inquiry found that only thirteen brakes had been applied instead of the twenty required to hold the train on the steep gradient. As it gathered speed, some passengers jumped clear but Esther, who was in one of the last two coaches, was fatally injured along with another passenger who died later in the day from his injuries.

THE OFFICIAL OPENING of a redevelopment scheme in 1970 heralded the replacement of these workers' houses with modern homes on Grange Road. On the first view, we are looking up the street from the same position as the original, so the long terraced row on the right would have run through the dwelling whose gable wall faces us. Original setts have survived in the road and the garden wall around The Grange is on the left of the picture. The second view is taken as if from behind the long terrace – this would have run left to right along the top edge of the lawned area at the front of the photograph. In the middle distance, the top of the church tower of St John

the Evangelist rises above the house with the white door and car. Its foundation stone of 18 June 1870 was laid by Edward Whitworth of The Grange, the chimneys and roof of which can be seen over the rooftops to the left.

MASSEY CROFT, WHITWORTH

WHITWORTH RAILWAY STATION on its single platform. The principal reason for extending
the railway line from Rochdale, through Whitworth, to Bacup was to carry stone away from
the local quarries and the line just visible in the bottom right of the picture ran into the
goods shed. Local stone was used for the foundations of the Eiffel Tower. Royal assent for the
line from Rochdale to Shawforth was given in 1862, but long negotiations with landowners,
who demanded high compensation for their land, delayed commencement of the work
until August 1865 after the tender had been accepted for £82,500. Contracts for Facit and

Whitworth Stations were not signed until March 1868. The line from Rochdale to Facit opened for goods traffic on 1 October 1870 and a month later for passenger traffic.

MASSEY CROFT AND the lawn to the right now occupy the site. The garden boundary wall appears on the left of the old photograph and ran along the course of the railway line from the bridge on Hall Street. The Bacup to Rochdale route was closed to passenger traffic on 16 June 1947, ostensibly because of a national fuel shortage. Goods traffic continued, but gradually decreased until the railway closed completely on 21 August 1967. However, the goods yard continued to be used by a local coal merchant who received supplies by road. Cowm Park Way was built on the track bed as far as Station Road which was the site of Facit Station. The lawn belongs to Riddiough Court, a sheltered housing complex of twenty-seven flats for elderly residents built in 1988. On the middle left of the picture is the former United Methodist Chapel on Market Street. It opened in 1878, but the congregation moved to new premises in January 1990 and it has recently been refurbished as private apartments.

If you enjoyed this book, you may also be interested in...

Around Rossendale

SUSAN HALSTEAD

This selection of over 200 wonderful old photographs of Rossendale show a differen world from the one we know today. Here are scenes of streets, buildings and local indu as they were but also many more showing people going about their everyday lives a home or school, visiting family-run shops, and enjoying their leisure time activities. The book will delight all who have grown up in the area as well as giving a younge generation, and newcomers, a glimpse of how Rossendale was just a short while ag

978 1 84588 3997

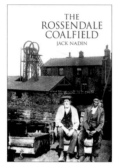

The Rossendale Coalfield

JACK NADIN

Coal mining is the second oldest industry in Britain after agriculture. As big coalm developed to feed the Industrial Revolution, many small moorland pits were still worked to provide fuel for local markets. These private coal mines were often wo on a shoestring budget, and the miners themselves toiled in extreme conditions u methods of mining hundreds of years old. Illustrated with over fifty images, this is a lasting record of the East Lancashire Coalfields.

978 0 7524 6112 0

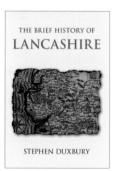

A Brief History of Lancashire

STEPHEN DUXBURY

Racing through the history of Lancashire, with Neolithic residents, Romans, Civil War victories and Victorians – and, of course, a few cotton mills along the way – delightful book will tell you everything you ought to know about the dramatic an fascinating history of the county – and a few things you never thought you woul

978 0 7524 6288 2

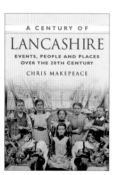

A Century of Lancashire

CHRIS MAKEPEACE

This fascinating selection of photographs illustrates the extraordinary transforma that has taken place in Lancashire during the twentieth century. The book offers insight into the daily lives and living conditions of local people and gives the rea glimpses and details of familiar places during a century of unprecedented chang

978 0 7509 4915 6

Visit our website and discover thousands of other History Press books.

www.thehistorypress.co.uk